Advance Praise
Democratic Rules of Order

Stuck in Dysfunction-ville? Are your meetings inefficient, frustrating and possibly not legal? *Democratic Rules of Order* is a small, brilliant book that can make a world of difference. Buy everyone a copy — it will be one of the best investments you've ever made.

—Bruce Batchelor, author, publisher, innovator, and no-longer-frustrated meeting attendee

This is *Robert's Rules*, simplified, modernized, clarified and, most importantly, humanized.

—Ric Getter, PCC Media Production/PCC-TV, Educational Advisory Council Membership chair, Portland Community College — Sylvania

Many condominiums get tangled up with *Robert's Rules of Order* which is most often far too complex. That is why the Team and VISOA recommend the uncomplicated *Democratic Rules of Order* to all stratas.

—David Grubb, board member and chair, Strata Support Team, Vancouver Island Strata Owners Association (VISOA)

We highly recommend this book to any organization for its clear and simple directions.

—Caroline Holm, clerk, First Church of Christ,

T0108427

Easy-to-follow guidelines allowed us to get a handle on the tasks that needed doing, without regularly digressing into chaos. Kudos to the authors for keeping a rowdy bunch of us on track.

—Pieter Vorster, Courtenay rugby team board member, and chief editor, TideChange.ca

I bought a copy for each member of the board and we voted to make it the official procedure manual. It's: 1) easy to understand, 2) easy to learn, 3) user-friendly, 4) logical, and 5) efficient.

—Edward E. Douglas, BA, MA, past vice-president of a library board of trustees

Truly the guide for the rest of us…with elegant solutions to three challenges: how to run meetings with fairness, efficiency, and good order, how to do so with rules that everybody can understand, and how to foster true democracy in a world that needs it more than ever.

—Jim Rietmulder, author, *When Kids Rule the School*, and co-founder, The Circle School

A gem of a reference book, it is practical, well-structured and is detailed and informative about meeting terminology.

—Gerry O'Sullivan, facilitator, mediator, and trainer, and author, *The Mediator's Toolkit*

10th Edition

Democratic Rules of Order

EASY-TO-USE RULES
FOR MEETINGS OF ANY SIZE

Fred Francis • Peg Francis

new society
PUBLISHERS

Dedicated to democracy

Cover design by Diane McIntosh.
Cover images ©iStock 683605452
First printing May 2019. New Catalyst edition April 2024.

Inquiries regarding requests to reprint all or part of
Democratic Rules of Order should be addressed to New Society
Publishers at the address below. To order directly from
the publishers, please call 1-250-247-9737, or order online at
www.newsociety.com

Any other inquiries can be directed by mail to:
New Society Publishers P.O. Box 189, Gabriola Island, BC
V0R 1X0, Canada
(250) 247-9737

LIBRARY AND ARCHIVES CANADA CATALOGUING IN
PUBLICATION
Title: Democratic rules of order : easy-to-use rules for
    meetings of any size / Fred Francis, Peg Francis.
Names: Francis, Fred, author. | Francis, Peg, author.
Description: 10th edition. | Includes index.
Identifiers: Canadiana (print) 20190060735 | Canadiana
    (ebook) 20190060743 | ISBN 9780865719064
    (softcover) | ISBN 9781550926996 (PDF) |
    ISBN 9781771422956 (EPUB)
Subjects: LCSH: Parliamentary practice—Handbooks,
    manuals, etc. | LCSH: Meetings—Handbooks, manuals, etc.
Classification: LCC JF515 .F73 2019 | DDC 060.4/2—dc23

Funded by the   Financé par le
Government   gouvernement
of Canada   du Canada

Canada

New Society Publishers' mission is to publish books that
contribute in fundamental ways to building an ecologically
sustainable and just society, and to do so with the least
possible impact on the environment, in a manner that
models this vision.

Certified

(B) Corporation

new society
PUBLISHERS

Contents

Foreword

Fred and Peg Francis have done an amazing job. Their book is absolutely indispensable for anyone who conducts meetings or participates in democratic discussion at any level—from parliamentary assemblies to condominium annual meetings. What the Francises have succeeded in doing is cutting through the forbidding complexities of running a meeting and reducing them to a simple set of common-sense rules that anyone can follow. When this book is employed, the disappointments that accompany many meetings can be sharply reduced and democratic participation greatly improved.

Over the years, I have chaired or attended hundreds of meetings at the governmental, business, church, and social levels and have often been frustrated by the difficulties of properly presiding over such meetings so that everyone can understand the process, and the will of the majority can be formulated and prevail. Much of the difficulty arises from the fact that few have the time or inclination to study the old-style rule books, and are therefore easily intimidated—even tyrannized sometimes—by the very few who know them.

The Francises' book is making an important contribution to democracy. It can be readily adopted by any group, council, union, or corporation, and will be of lasting benefit. Speaking personally, I have sat through years of parliamentary debate and appreciate the value—and necessity—of achieving consensus in a democratic proceeding by having rules and following them. Up until now, the rules have been exceedingly complex, often confusing, and unsatisfactory at many levels. From here on in, those groups who adopt *Democratic Rules of Order* will find significant improvement in both the tenor of their meetings and the validity of the results.

Douglas Leiterman was Parliamentary Correspondent for Southam News, an Executive Producer at CBC, and CEO of Motion Picture Bond Company.

Preface

Are you frustrated by meetings that lack efficiency … fail to move smoothly through an agenda … lose order and professionalism due to emotional outbursts … or do not foster constructive decision-making that truly represents the wishes of the membership?

You're not alone. And it doesn't have to be that way!

After years of volunteering their time for community groups—including attending hundreds of professional and nonprofit meetings—Fred and Peg Francis recognized the need for a concise, authoritative resource to assist boards of directors, committees, and other organized groups seeking to fairly represent their memberships by hosting efficient, effective meetings.

Because they could not find such a resource, they created one. It took several years of refining (and a great deal of input from executives, parliamentarians, and other users) to perfect the rules, to be sure that each point was crystal clear, and that not a single necessary rule was missing. Introduced in 1994 as *Distinctly Democratic Rules of Order* (changed to *Democratic Rules of Order* in later printings), this easy-to-use book has become a respected and valued reference for thousands of organizations, large and small, and for students being taught the democratic process in classrooms around the world.

Used By Diverse Groups

From unions and professional associations to strata councils, churches, and nongovernmental organizations, *Democratic Rules of Order* is a "pocket guide" setting out a step-by-step process that allows all members to participate in the exchange of ideas and group decision-making, including virtual meetings.

The book can be read in less than an hour and is intentionally small, so it is easy to carry to meetings for on-the-spot reference when a question arises.

Easy-to-use Format

To make it easy to follow, the book is divided into two parts. *Part 1: The Rules* describes organizational structures and members' roles, and it includes step-by-step procedures for handling the most critical part of any meeting: the decision-making process. It helps the reader navigate through the democratic processes of:

- introducing ideas
- making motions and amendments
- handling points of order and disturbances
- managing the voting process
- working on and with committees.

Part 2: Further Help provides additional important reference information, including:

- frequently asked questions
- a scripted example of a meeting that uses all the key elements of *Democratic Rules of Order*
- a flowchart that illustrates the rules of order
- a summary of the rules of order for quick reference during a meeting.

Since 1996, this book has been a best seller in Canada. By reaching a wider audience with this 10th edition, the authors hope to improve the world, one meeting and one decision at a time.

PART 1

The Rules

Introduction

Fairness and Orderliness

These parliamentary rules of order help people to deliberate and consider ideas together, and then make decisions as wisely, fairly, and easily as possible. These rules are relevant for meetings of any size that are undivided by organized political parties. Ideally, decisions are based on objective consideration of facts, unaffected by emotions, group pressures, or unnecessary protocols. The purpose of this book is to help your organization reach this ideal.

Democratic Principles

This book is not an abridged version of other books. It is a complete set of rules determined by common practice and the natural laws of democracy—"rule by the ruled," as Webster's dictionary puts it. These self-evident principles, when applied to decision-making meetings, include:

- **the right of each individual member** to participate equally and fully in orderly meetings that are free from intimidation, filibustering, and other disturbances and in which all members will follow the same easily understood rules, including the right to be equally and fully informed of all events, whether a member is present or not
- **the right of the majority of members** to make the decisions.

A Democratic Ideal

We should remember that we all belong to the same organization, with a common purpose. We can have widely differing views and still work together for a common good without dividing into opposing sides, each trying to get its own way. The best decisions are made when we listen thoughtfully to the information being presented and then make our own decisions privately.

Another Democratic Ideal

Must we accept a legal decision if it is a bad one? Yes and no. Yes, because, to practice democracy, we must accept the decision and do what it requires us to do. No, because we are not required to change our opinion. At some later date, the opportunity may occur for a review of the decision or we may even find that the decision was good after all!

Degrees of Formality

In small or close-knit groups, decisions can often be made by consensus or general agreement, provided that the chair or secretary recording each decision is sure that most members agree (**see pages 15, Informal Chair, and 37, Less Formality**).

Large groups, too, often make decisions informally. The mover's privilege (**see page 19, Mover's Privilege**) allows cooperative members to work out decisions quickly and easily. A more formal amending process is automatically required if opinions are divided. The degree of formality is usually determined by custom, agreement, or a law as defined in the next paragraph.

Higher Laws

Rules of order are automatically overruled when a law of the land, a constitution, a bylaw, or an existing standing rule applies.

Throughout this book, we refer to any of these as a *law.*

Rules of order apply to the conduct of meetings only. They do not interpret laws or make up for deficiencies in bylaws or standing rules.

Minority Rights

While a democratic majority rule system may appear to be in conflict with minority rights, remember that there are higher laws that protect minority and individual rights. Nearly all nations have laws that protect the natural rights of all individuals, including the UN's Universal Declaration of Human Rights (UDHR). No group may make a decision that would violate universally recognized human rights and fundamental freedoms.

For Maximum Efficiency

Sharing the decision-making process in meetings is like driving a car. There are rules to be learned and skills to be attained. Once this has been done, group decision-making is second nature, like driving. If each member reads this book thoughtfully at least once, and if the chair does the same at least twice, and if members agree to follow these rules, your meetings should move as easily as the car of an experienced driver who can drive competently without wondering which pedal to press.

The Tenth Edition

The tenth edition, like each previous edition, has been revised to make the book clearer, more useful, and easier to work with. However, the rules of all editions are so similar that organizations can use earlier editions along with the latest edition without conflicts.

Virtual Meetings

These rules, modified if necessary, can be used for telephone or video conference meetings and for computer-connected meetings in which discussions and voting are done electronically.

To Adopt or Modify These Rules of Order

Add to the standing rules or bylaws a statement such as: "This organization's meetings shall be governed by *Democratic Rules of Order*." You could also add: "Members' general meetings shall be conducted by a formal chair, and the executive board's meetings shall be conducted by an informal chair" (**see pages 14 and 15, Formal Chair and Informal Chair**). Similarly, modifications can be made to these rules to make them conform to an organization's special needs.

An Impersonal Referee

These rules are complete. When adopted, they form the official rules of order for your organization's meetings. This book is your parliamentarian—or referee—when needed.

Governing Elements

Good governance has structure.

Government Control

The governments of some jurisdictions require that the constitution and bylaws of incorporated societies be approved by the members and that reports be submitted annually.

Constitution

A constitution is a short document stating the name and purpose of the organization. Changes to a constitution may require advance notice, a large majority of votes (e.g. two-thirds or three-quarters), a secret ballot, and/or government approval if the organization is incorporated. Indeed, some clauses may be unalterable, so an organization might have to be disbanded and reformed to change them. Many unincorporated organizations today are formed without constitutions and place all governing rules in their bylaws.

Bylaws

The governing rules of the organization, covering topics such as membership, officers, elections, duties, finances, meetings, quorum, discipline, amendments, and the seal. Changes to the bylaws may require advance notice, a large majority of votes (e.g. two-thirds or three-quarters), a secret ballot, and/or government approval.

Standing Rules

Standing rules are a record, usually in list form, of previously made decisions that provide future guidance. Standing rules can be changed by a majority of votes at any regular meeting, provided a quorum (the minimum number of members required to be present, **see page 15, Quorum**) is present.

Unless all members are present and none object, changes to an existing standing rule governing the conduct of members' meetings apply only to future meetings. Some organizations require advance notice before a decision listed in the standing rules can be changed (**see page 50, Q17**).

Rules of Order

A set of rules, established by the standing rules or bylaws, by which the members agree to govern their meetings. This book supplies a complete set of rules that can be used by any organized group. Rules of order are subject always to the laws of the land, the constitution, the bylaws, and existing standing rules, any of which we call a *law* in this book.

Executive Board

A group of members elected for a limited time to conduct the organization's business in accordance with the members' wishes. Their responsibilities and limitations are specified in the bylaws. Their authority lies only with the whole board, and no single member should assume any special authority or responsibility unless such powers have been delegated to that individual by the board. When a person serves in a capacity such as "Director," "Strata Council Member," "Trustee," or "Governor," that person is still obligated to act in complete compliance with the will of the members.

Officers

President, vice president, secretary, treasurer, etc., elected by the members or appointed by the executive board for a limited time. Their responsibilities and limitations are specified in the bylaws. In some organizations, the officers form part or all of the executive board.

Election Procedures

Usually found in the bylaws and stating when elections are to be held, the requirements and terms of office, nominating and voting procedures, balloting, and the number and appointment of vote counters.

Members Making Decisions

It is easier to make good decisions when everyone knows the rules.

Final Authority

Given a quorum, the will of the majority of members present and voting at any meeting held in accordance with the bylaws is the final authority and cannot be thwarted by any individual or by any previous decision, except where a higher law provides an exception (**see page 5, Higher Laws**).

Equal Rights

Unless a law states differently, each member has one vote and an equal voice in all decisions.

The Chair

The president or someone elected by the members or appointed by the executive board to conduct the members' meetings.

Chair's Authority

The chair's duty is to preserve order and fairness in meetings by following the bylaws and rules of order. Members must abide by the rulings of the chair without debate except when a point of order (**see page 32, Point of Order**) is made.

Formal Chair

In large meetings, the chair must be—and must be seen to be—absolutely impartial. The chair must refrain from expressing personal opinions in words or gestures and should not participate in discussion except to guide it in an orderly fashion. If, on rare occasions, the chair has relevant, brief information, the chair may depart from this rule, but the chair must always avoid showing any bias. The chair cannot make a motion.

If the chair needs to participate actively in a discussion, arrangements should be made for another member to fill this position until the motion has been voted on. A member may call the chair to a point of order for wrongful participation, and the chair should comply with good spirit (**see page 58, Q31**).

Informal Chair

In smaller or less formal meetings, members may have a bylaw, standing rule, or custom permitting the chair to participate in discussions with the same privileges as other members.

Addressing the Chair

Members must wait for permission (a verbal or nonverbal sign) from the chair before speaking. If several members stand at once, the chair selects one and notes who should be next. The others should sit until the speaker has finished; in large assemblies, the chair may require members wishing to speak to line up behind a microphone, or put their names on a list and wait their turn. A list of the order of speakers, preferably visible to all, is often useful, especially for virtual meetings.

Quorum

The minimum number of members required by a law to be present before decisions can be made at meetings. The chair must find out if a quorum is present before the meeting begins and be kept informed of any drop in numbers that might cause the loss of a quorum. The chair should warn the members if this is likely to occur. If a quorum is not present, the meeting may continue unofficially and should arrange, if possible, to get a quorum or to set the time of the next meeting.

Agenda

The items of business and the order in which they are to be discussed at meetings, generally prepared by the secretary with executive board approval, or, in smaller meetings, by the chair. The agenda should be made known to members beforehand. An agenda distributed in advance is particularly valuable for virtual meetings. The agenda can be changed by the members any time during the meeting except when another motion is on the floor (being considered by the members). The agenda change must be voted on if one or more members object. Agenda headings might include:

- Opening of the meeting and approval of the agenda
- Minutes of the previous meeting
- Correspondence and reports
- Business arising from minutes, correspondence, and reports
- Motions to be presented and new business
- Announcements
- Adjournment and closing

Motions and Decisions

Sometimes decisions are made by consensus in which the chair says "If there are no objections, then [the decision is described]," but otherwise all decisions are made with motions or resolutions (see page 55, Q26) in which a member says "I move [that some action be taken]." Before any motion can be considered, it must be seconded by another member; this prevents time being spent discussing an idea that has little chance of approval.

A new motion cannot be made until the motion on the floor has been withdrawn or voted on, except for those motions that directly affect the motion on the floor. Possible actions that would affect the motion on the floor would include:

- amendment to a motion (see page 20, Amendments)
- postponement to a later date (see page 21, postpone)
- referral to another entity (see page 21, referr)
- imposing a limit to speakers' time (see page 22, under Voting)
- making changes to the voting procedure (see page 22, under Voting)
- point of order (see page 32, Point of Order)

Unless a law specifically allows, a member must be present to make a motion, thus preserving the valuable mover's privilege. If the members have been notified already of a proposed motion, however, any member present can make the motion when it comes up on the agenda.

If the motion is clear, does not conflict with a law, and has been seconded, the chair or the secretary should read out the motion to make sure it is recorded correctly. Experienced movers sometimes have motions already written to give to the secretary. If possible, the motion should be worded affirmatively.

It is customary to allow the mover to speak to the motion first, and then again at the end of the discussion.

Notice of motion

A notice of motion can be made to members in writing or verbally during a meeting regarding a motion to be presented at a future meeting.

Special meeting

Unless a law states differently, those present at a special meeting can make decisions only on topics given in the notice calling that meeting.

Opinion poll (straw vote)

A nonbinding opinion poll (straw vote) can be held by the chair any time during a meeting if the members are willing. If a member objects, the chair should ask the members for a decision and conduct the opinion poll or not according to the members' vote (**see page 55, Q27**).

Mover's Privilege

During discussion, ideas for improving the motion may occur. Provided that not more than one member objects, the mover may reword or withdraw the motion any time before it has been voted on. A seconder for new wording or withdrawal is required. Rewording can be continued until the motion is as perfect as the mover, assisted by the meeting, can make it.

Once the mover has decided on new wording—and it has been seconded—the chair or secretary should read out the reworded motion, which immediately becomes a new motion on the floor, replacing the previous

one. If two members object prior to this reading out of the reworded motion, changes can
be made only with motions to amend.

Amendments

If the mover does not—or cannot, because of
objections—make a suggested change to the
motion, any member may move an amendment to the original motion. An amendment
may delete, substitute, or add words that will
modify the original motion but must not
negate it or change the intent.

The amendment, when accepted by the
chair and seconded, immediately becomes
a new motion on the floor, temporarily
replacing the original motion. The amendment grants mover's privilege to the mover
of the amendment. Any rewording must
be acceptable to the chair as not changing the topic. The details of the proposed
amendment are discussed (not the original
motion), and then the amendment is voted
on. An amendment cannot be amended, but
it can be defeated and replaced with another
amendment.

If the amendment passes, the secretary
should read the newly amended motion,

which is now a new motion on the floor to be discussed (if desired) and voted on. It cannot be reworded or withdrawn by the mover's privilege now, since it has been partly established by the members, but this new motion can be passed, defeated, or amended again.

If the amendment fails, the previous motion again becomes the motion on the floor. If this previous motion was the original motion (having never been amended), then the original mover regains the mover's privilege. Further amendments are allowed, one at a time.

Postpone, Refer

A member may, any time before the motion has been voted on, move to **postpone** the motion on the floor (including any amendments passed) to an indefinite or a specific future occasion or to **refer** it to a standing committee, or an ad hoc committee specific for this purpose, for further study.

A member believing that consideration of a particular motion would be unwise could move "that we postpone the motion indefinitely." If the motion to **postpone**

indefinitely is seconded and passed, then that particular motion cannot be discussed further at that meeting. It can be brought up at another meeting. A motion cannot be postponed permanently, because one meeting cannot bind a future meeting.

Voting

When all members who wish to speak have done so, the chair should call for a vote. Unless a larger majority is required (**see page 25, Larger Majority Vote**), a decision is made (the motion is passed) when a quorum is present and more than half the votes are affirmative. Spoiled ballots and members not voting are not counted (**see page 51, Q18**).

Calling for a vote

Members who believe discussion is complete sometimes call out "We are ready to vote," or the chair might ask "Are you ready to vote?" The response is a guide for the chair only and does not force a vote. A member who believes that the chair is calling for the vote too early or is delaying too long can rise on a point of order (**see page 32, Point of Order**) and move

that "we delay the vote for more discussion"
or that "we vote now." Such a motion needs
seconding and should be voted on with little
or no discussion.

Member's right to speak

Every member has a right to speak once to a
motion, but in large meetings, a motion limiting speakers' times could be passed. The chair
should not normally accept a motion to "vote
now" if members who have not yet spoken
are waiting to do so. However, if arguments
on both sides of the question have been fairly
presented and good order is being jeopardized
by discussions becoming repetitive, the chair
should accept such a motion.

After the members have decided to vote,
either by general consensus or by passing a
motion to vote, the chair or the secretary
should read out the motion again, and the
chair should make sure that all members
understand it. Then the chair should call for
the vote with "All in favor of the motion,
please say 'yes' [or raise a hand]" (pause), "All
opposed, say 'no' [or raise a hand]," or "Please
mark your ballots now," etc. The chair must
announce the result. If ballots need to be

counted, the chair announces the results after the ballots are tallied.

How votes are taken

Custom or a standing rule usually determines how votes are taken. Some groups vote by voice, which makes it more difficult to tell which way others are voting; some groups vote by a show of hands, voting cards, standing, secret ballot, or roll call (**see page 55, Q25**), all of which make it easier to count the votes. If the chair, assisted by the secretary, is uncertain which way the vote went, the chair can ask for a show of hands. If it is still unclear, the chair can ask for a standing vote, saying "Those in favor, please stand" (pause), "Please be seated. Those opposed, please stand" (pause), "Please be seated."

A member who believes that there has been a **miscount** can ask—or, if necessary, move—"that we repeat the count with a standing [or ballot] vote." If this motion is seconded and passed, then the vote must be taken again. Motions can be made requiring that a vote be by ballot, that the counted ballots be destroyed, that the number of votes for and against be announced, or that some other action be taken regarding the vote.

Absentee voting

Unless a law specifically allows proxy or absentee voting, a member must be present to vote, either in person or virtually.

Ethics

A member who would benefit personally from a decision may participate in the discussion but should voluntarily refrain from voting.

Tie Vote

A tie vote means the motion has not passed. Members might wish to reconsider it immediately, or at a future time. In some organizations, an already existing law gives the chair an extra vote to break a tie.

Larger Majority Vote

A mover who believes that the action being proposed needs strong support from many members may finish the motion with wording such as: "… and that this motion require a three-quarters [or some other ratio] affirmative vote to pass." A simple majority of members could easily remove this special requirement with an amendment; therefore, if this restriction is not removed through an amendment, the larger majority vote requirement has been accepted by the meeting and is now needed for the motion to pass. Sometimes a law will already exist requiring a larger majority vote on certain financial matters, bylaw changes, or other matters of import.

Informal Discussion

Occasionally, there is merit in discussing an idea informally before a motion has been formulated. To allow for this, a member may move "that we discuss [some topic] informally for a few minutes." This motion needs seconding and should be voted on almost immediately. After discussing the topic, if no motion is forthcoming, the meeting should proceed with the next item on the agenda.

Rescind

Unless a law makes an exception, and providing it would not create a breach of contract, a motion to rescind (repeal) a previous decision requires only a majority to pass and can be made at a time when the agenda allows (normally under new business or resulting from a point of order changing the agenda).

Reconsider

A motion to reconsider a previous decision can be made immediately after the decision has been made or at any meeting during new business or when it has been put on the agenda (perhaps by a point of order). It should be voted on immediately with little or no discussion. If the motion to reconsider is passed, then a member moves the previous motion or a replacement motion on the same topic, and it is again discussed and voted on. The mover's privilege (**see page 19, Mover's Privilege**) applies. The new decision replaces the previous one. A motion can be reconsidered as often as the members are willing (**see page 70**). Once the decision to reconsider has been made, no new business can be done until the reconsideration has been dealt with.

Minutes

Minutes are records of meetings, kept by the secretary. They should include at least all major events and motions (**see page 46, Q7**). The secretary should maintain a filing system for minutes, reports, correspondence, etc.

After the minutes of the previous meeting have been circulated or read to all members,

the chair should ask if there are any corrections. After any corrections have been made,
the chair should ask "All in favor of adopting
the minutes as circulated [or read, or correct-
ed], please say 'yes' [or raise a hand]" (pause),
"All opposed, please say 'no' [or raise a hand]"
and then announce the decision. Once adopted, and signed by the chair and secretary, the
minutes are an official record generally acceptable in a court of law.

Reports

Executive boards, committees, and individuals
often report recommendations or give other
information to the members at meetings.

After a report containing information has
been read to the meeting, no motion is necessary. However, in some groups it is customary
to finish with "I move that this report be
received as read," which means that the members have heard and understood the report.

If the report contains a recommendation,
the person presenting the report might move
that "this report be **adopted** as read." This
motion means that the members have agreed
with and adopted the report and its recommendations. Of course, a member could

propose an amendment changing "adopted" to "received," so that the members would not be bound by the report's recommendations. Treasurers' reports are usually received, rather than adopted, as the members are not in a position to guarantee the report's accuracy.

Ratifying a Previous Decision

If a decision was made, perhaps due to an emergency, that exceeded the authority of the member, committee, or meeting at the time it was made, this decision can be either ratified or not by the members who do have the authority at a later meeting (**see page 57, Q29**). This is done by a member making a motion to ratify the decision. Normally, the motion to ratify is quickly passed. However, if the motion to ratify is not passed, this is a **non-confidence** vote. Unless a higher law (e.g. a bylaw) has provided for this in a different way, the member or group that made the decision in question must resign and an election be called to have them replaced.

Adjournment

If a bylaw or standing rule requires adjournment by a specified time, the chair should warn the members as that time draws near, so that they can either finish quickly or extend the meeting with a motion, if it is allowed. If the meeting has not been extended, the chair should declare the meeting adjourned at the specified time. Otherwise, the chair could say, "Since the business is finished, if there are no objections" (pause), "the meeting is adjourned." Or the chair could say, "Since the business is finished, let's adjourn; all in favor, please say 'yes' " (pause), "All opposed, please say 'no.' " If the motion passes, the chair then says "The meeting is adjourned."

Keeping Meetings Flowing

A productive meeting needs good order.

Staying on the Subject

Members must discuss only one topic or motion at a time. If necessary, the chair should interrupt a speaker to insist that this rule be obeyed. If ideas are brought up that may be valuable but are off topic, a "Parking Lot" concept can be used. The chair or secretary records the ideas to be brought up later for discussion at an appropriate time, perhaps as a new business agenda item for a future meeting.

More Thought, Less Talk

A member must not take more than a fair share of floor time nor speak more than once on a motion until all others who wish to do so have had a turn. Exceptions may occur, however, with new information or a series of questions and answers involving useful facts.

If necessary, members could pass a motion or have a standing rule, starting next meeting (**see page 10, Standing Rules**), limiting each speaker's time and appointing a timekeeper to enforce it.

Mutual Respect

Members must respect the rights of other members to have their own quiet judgment on issues. Decisions should be based on consideration of facts rather than on the skill of the speakers or one person's opinion of how others should vote. Members should speak to contribute light only, not heat!

Members must not use any form of personal criticism or ridicule to sway opinions. A member may criticize an idea, but never a fellow member. A member must never interject or interfere with another member's right to an uninterrupted floor when speaking, except as allowed under a point of order. The chair should insist that this rule be followed.

Point of Order

A member who believes that a law or the meeting's good order is being breached may rise at any time and say, "Mister/Madam

Chair, point of order." The chair should immediately acknowledge this member, who should then briefly explain why he or she believes a law or good order is being breached. The chair then rules on the point, either correcting the situation or explaining why it is in order.

If the chair declares that the situation is in order, the member may exercise **one last option** by rising and saying "Mister/Madam Chair, I request a vote on this point of order." First the member, and then the chair, briefly explain their reasons. Then with little or no further discussion, the chair calls for a vote, saying "All who believe that [this action] conforms to our rules [or good order], please say 'yes' [or raise a hand]" (pause), "Those who disagree, please say 'no' [or raise a hand]." The chair and the member raising the point of order must abide by this vote.

Disturbances

Filibustering (intentionally delaying progress by prolonged speaking) or any other action that interferes with good order is not allowed. If a member is speaking too long, the chair should give a polite reminder. If the member continues, the chair can interrupt and request a decision from the meeting with "I request a decision from the meeting. All wishing this member to stop speaking now, please say 'yes' [or raise a hand]" (pause), "All opposed, please say 'no' [or raise a hand]." If the decision was for the member to stop speaking, the chair says, "Sir/Madam, the members wish you to stop speaking now. Please do so." Or if the decision was opposed, "Sir/Madam, the members are willing for you to continue. Please do so."

If a member or group of members does not stop speaking when asked by the chair or a motion has been passed by the members, then the chair can interrupt the speaker and ask for a motion requiring the speaker(s) to leave the meeting or, if necessary, for a motion to adjourn the meeting to reconvene at a later time. Only the members can make such a decision. Physical force should not be used against a member, although the speaker's microphone could be turned off on request of the chair (**see page 43, Q2, and page 44, Q3**).

Differing Opinions

If there is a difference over the meaning of a bylaw or a procedure, etc., the chair may assist in solving the dispute. For example, the chair could pose a question designed to resolve the dispute and ask for a show of hands on it. The final decision rests with the members (**see example, page** 74).

A New Chair

Serving as chair need not be a dreaded job; the rules in this book are straightforward, and your fellow members can assist you, if needed. You can let it be known that you appreciate help. Ask members to call out if they can't hear you and to remind you if you forget something. You could suggest "If you see ways I can chair the meetings more efficiently, please ask the secretary to give me a copy of the rules of order in which you have highlighted the points I most need to review."

As well as studying the bylaws, standing rules, and rules of order beforehand, it is helpful to study the agenda and perhaps to annotate it with reminders and notes so you won't forget them during the meeting. By the way, starting meetings on time is a valuable habit.

Committees and Small Meetings

Meetings can be both informal and orderly.

Committees

A committee is a group of one or more persons appointed by the executive board or the members to perform a continuing or short-term function. A **standing committee** is permanent until disbanded, although its membership may be changed periodically. An **ad hoc committee** is appointed to do a specific task and is temporary. The chair of a committee is appointed by the members or the executive board, or is elected from within the committee. Unless otherwise stated, the quorum of a committee or meeting is a majority of its members. Written guidelines are often used to provide order and continuity.

Less Formality

In committees and small meetings, the chair participates informally as a leader

(see page 15, Informal Chair)—subject always to the law and the will of the meeting, which in turn is responsible to the appointing body. The following is a list of examples of meeting types, in order of increasing degrees of formality:

- work parties making decisions by consensus led by the chair
- small meetings making minor decisions by consensus that are announced by the chair and recorded in minutes
- meetings of executive boards with an agenda and motions that are seconded, voted on, announced by the chair, and recorded in minutes by a secretary.

Special Committees

Most committees are democratic, but sometimes a nondemocratic committee is formed in which one person has full responsibility, although others may help.

Chairing a Committee Meeting

Ideally, a committee brings to bear upon a subject the combined experience and wisdom of several people. But sometimes well-meaning people talk too much or too forcefully, quite unaware of how much time this wastes and how unfair it is to others. Meetings must be protected from such imbalance. The chair should not allow any member to be overly dominant.

The chair should assist members in sticking to the business at hand. (Socializing can be done before or after the meeting.) Light good humor is great, but should be brief. Replies to divergent opinions should be controlled and not allowed to degenerate into arguments. Facts should be allowed to speak for them selves. A little silence during a meeting—as members ponder a situation—is often the sign of an effective group.

When an idea needs to be written down or a letter produced, most committees find that these are better written and corrected by one or two people and then presented to the whole committee for final review.

In all meetings—of any size—the ideal is for members to seek the best solutions *together, as a unit,* rather than having sides debate to have their own viewpoints adopted. (True for legislative assemblies too, if only they applied it!)

Nondemocratic Meetings

Some meetings (such as a sales meeting in which a manager is instructing personnel) are not intended to be democratic, yet orderliness and respect for every individual and the employment of the basic principles of democratic rules will improve the efficiency of any meeting. Including a little democratic decision-making, when possible, usually brightens a meeting, making it more interesting for all participants.

PART 2

Further Help

Frequently Asked Questions

Involving the Chair

Q1. *What qualities does the chair most need?*

A1. Self-control, good humor, and a thorough knowledge of the constitution, the bylaws, the standing rules, and the rules of order of the organization.

Q2. *What can a chair do to ensure a fair and harmonious discussion of a contentious item?*

A2. If necessary, the chair can remind members:

- that the rules by which they have agreed to be governed allow them to discuss and make joint decisions in an orderly fashion, even when opinions are strongly divided

- that a member's right to an uninterrupted floor includes freedom from any kind of audience response while that member is speaking

- that a member who has spoken once may not reply to other speakers' statements—no matter how outrageous—until all others who wish to speak have done so
- that a member must be acknowledged by the chair before speaking
- that we need not change our opinions, but we must accept the voting majority as the authorized decision-maker.

It may be helpful to have copies of this book on hand; members could be allowed to borrow one, and return it at the end of the meeting, so that appropriate sections can be referred to. If necessary, the chair should respectfully insist that these rules, especially those on **pages 31 to 35 (Keeping Meetings Flowing)**, be followed.

Q3. *How should the chair deal with confrontational, angry members?*

A3. The most effective way is to not react even a little, to be calm, objective, proactive, and aware that remaining polite and dispassionate will help keep the situation controlled. Compassion for people less able to control their emotions sometimes helps a chair from dropping to the same level. It gets easier with experience (**see page 33, Disturbances**).

Q4.   *Can the chair vote?*

A4.   Yes, unless a law states differently.

However, a formal chair (**see page 14, Formal Chair**) should do so as inconspicuously as possible to avoid showing bias.

Q5.   *If both the chair and the vice-chair are absent, what happens?*

A5.   Any member, perhaps the secretary, can call the meeting to order, call for nominations, and conduct an election of a temporary chair for that meeting (**see page 13, The Chair**).

Q6.   *Should the chair guide the discussion?*

A6.   An occasional verbal summary can be helpful, but a formal chair (**see page 14, Formal Chair**) must be careful to maintain impartiality.

A chair who keeps the discussion on track, prevents overzealous members from dominating, helps members speak clearly one at a time, and keeps the meeting from dragging on with repetitions, is doing much to make the meeting worthwhile. With direction from the chair, minor decisions can be made by consensus. For example, the chair might say, "Unless there is an objection, we will continue this meeting without the noisy microphone."

Involving the Secretary

Q7. *How detailed should minutes be?*

A7. As detailed as the secretary and/or the members wish. Minutes should contain all motions exactly as passed and a very brief description of all major actions. Minutes often look like expanded agendas. Minutes of formal meetings will generally be fuller than those of informal meetings. Minutes of informal meetings might be simply a dated list of events and decisions.

Q8. *Must the minutes include the names of the mover and seconder?*

A8. No, but in more formal meetings, the secretary may wish to include them, or the members could pass a motion requiring that this be done.

Q9. *Must the minutes of the previous meeting be read at the beginning of the meeting?*

A9. Not necessarily; if the minutes have already been circulated (either before the meeting or at the beginning of the meeting), members may not wish to have them read aloud. The members determine the agenda (**see page 16, Agenda**).

Q10. *When minutes of the previous meeting have been corrected, must the secretary rewrite them?*

A10. Normally, corrections are made in the text or margin of the secretary's copy of the minutes and initialed by the chair and the secretary. However, if the secretary wishes, or if the members pass such a motion, then the minutes should be rewritten and the new copy be signed by the chair and the secretary. For virtual meetings, the minutes may be signed and transmitted electronically with the date of changes noted.

Q11. *If the minutes of a previous meeting have been adopted and are later found to contain an error, what should be done?*

A11. Once a meeting's minutes have been adopted and signed, that signed copy cannot be changed. Corrections should be noted and approved by the members in the later meeting and included in that meeting's minutes. Then a note of the later correction should be made on, or attached to, the original minutes, dated, and signed by the chair and secretary. For virtual meetings, any corrections to minutes can be made electronically with the changes dated.

Q12. *Can a secretary make a motion?*

A12. Any member except a formal chair (**see page 14, Formal Chair**) can make a motion. However, in large meetings, it is usual for motions to be made from the floor.

Motions and Other Topics

Q13. *Can a motion be put on the agenda without naming a mover?*

A13. Yes. When its turn comes on the agenda, any member can move it. If the motion is not moved, the meeting proceeds on to the next item on the agenda (**see page 16, Agenda**).

Q14. *What are the advantages of the mover's privilege (see page 19, Mover's Privilege)?*

A14. When members are cooperative, the mover's privilege enables them to improve a motion in an easy, natural way. Efficiency increases with experience. Since objection from any two members requires a more formal amending process, this privilege cannot be abused.

Q15. *Can a member speak and vote against his or her own motion?*

A15. Yes. The only restrictions on members' participation are those on **pages 31 to 35 (Keeping Meetings Flowing)**. However, it may be wiser to modify the motion with the mover's privilege or an amendment (**see pages 17, under Motions and Decisions, and 19, Mover's Privilege**).

Q16. *Can a member who will be absent submit a written amendment to a motion that is on the agenda?*

A16. No, unless a higher law allows (**see page 5, Higher Laws**). However, the member

could submit a motion for the agenda
that addresses the issue. It would need
to be moved and seconded at the meeting to proceed (**see page 17, Motions
and Decisions**). In a virtual meeting,
the moving and seconding could be
done electronically. The absent member
would be made aware of the decision
through the minutes.

Q17. *Can the members add or change a standing rule during the meeting to give the
chair a tie-breaking vote?*

A17. No. They can change the standing rule,
but it will not take effect until the next
meeting because the meeting is governed by the existing standing rules.
This rule protects the right of members
not present at a particular meeting
from having a major rule changed
during that meeting—when they are
not there to participate in the decision.
However, if *all* members are present
and none object, a standing rule could
be changed immediately (**see page
10, Standing Rules, and page 25, Tie
Vote**).

Q18. *Our quorum is 40. Forty members were present. On a vote, there were eight affirmative votes, seven negative votes, and one spoiled ballot that did not contain a "yes" or a "no." Twenty-four members did not vote. Did the motion pass?*

A18. Yes. Two conditions are necessary for a motion to pass:

(1) The total number of members present must be at least a quorum.

(2) A majority of the legitimate votes cast must be affirmative.

In this case, both conditions were met. A quorum of members was present. The spoiled ballot did not count. Eight votes were a majority of the 15 legitimate votes cast (**see page 22, Voting**).

Q19. *What if a member feels an intermission would be helpful?*

A19. The member can raise a point of order (**see page 32, Point of Order**) and move that members take a break and reassemble at a stated time.

Q20. *Can an agenda be changed during a meeting to include a particular topic considered earlier?*

A20. Yes. At a convenient time, a member can raise a point of order (assuming the proposed change will improve the good order of the meeting) and move the change in the agenda (**see page 16, Agenda**).

Q21. *When can a motion that has been post-poned indefinitely be brought up again?*

A21. At a future meeting, at a time when the agenda allows (normally under new business or resulting from a point of order changing the agenda).

Q22. *Our bylaws require a notice of motion in order to spend over $1,000 at any meeting. A notice of motion to install an electronic security system for $5,000 was properly sent to each member. During the meeting this motion was changed; the decision was made to purchase better locks instead, for $4,000. Is this acceptable?*

A22. Yes. The amount is within the financial limit established by the notice of motion, and the motion is on the same topic of security. If there were a difference of opinion on this, the chair could ask "If you agree with my decision to accept this motion as being in accord with the notice of motion, please raise your hand" (pause), "If opposed, please raise your hand," thereby emphasizing that the members are the final authority (**see page 34, Differing Opinions**).

However, changing the motion (by means of the mover's privilege or an amendment) to purchasing a system for $5,200 would *not* be acceptable, as the amount is over the limit established by the notice of motion. Similarly, changing the motion to purchasing a sound system for $5,000 would not be acceptable, as the topic is different.

Q23. *How can we have a relaxed, interactive "think tank" session, with maximum freedom to explore new, problem-solving ideas in an orderly way?*

A23. Use the informal discussion rule (**see page 26, Informal Discussion**) to free the meeting from formality. Then appoint the chair or a member to act as a neutral facilitator to be sure that every idea presented is received with complete absence of pre-judgment on its merit so that no one is reluctant to mention a "far-out" idea. You could also appoint the secretary or a member as a recorder to list the ideas on a board or chart so that none are lost.

Large meetings sometimes break into smaller groups, each with its own facilitator and recorder. When the session is finished, the groups come together and hear reports from the facilitators. Ideas originating from these sessions may lead to motions.

Q24. *Can you give an example of an acceptable and an unacceptable amendment?*

A24. Consider this motion: "I move that we go to Sam's restaurant next time."

Amendment #1: "I move that we amend this motion by replacing the word 'Sam's' with 'The Golden Pagoda.'" This is acceptable, because it does not negate the motion or change the topic.

Amendment #2: "I move that we amend this motion by adding the word 'not' in front of the word 'go.'" This is not acceptable, because it negates the original motion (**see page 20, Amendments**).

The same result could be achieved more simply by defeating the original motion.

Q25. *What is a vote by roll call?*

A25. The secretary calls the name of each member, who then votes audibly. Each member's vote is recorded on a list.

Q26. *What is a resolution?*

A26. A resolution is a formal expression of the meeting's opinion on some topic, or a resolve to take some action worded in a special way. It usually consists of a pre-amble containing one or more premises followed by a conclusion. For example: "I move that we adopt the following resolution: *Whereas* [followed by one or more premises], *therefore, be it resolved that* [followed by a resolve]." Of course, the members can change any part with the mover's privilege or amendments before voting on the whole motion.

Q27. *What is an example of an opinion poll (straw vote)?*

A27. While considering the purchase of a new computer, a member wanted to know how many members would make use of it and asked the chair to find out. The chair said "If there are no objections, we will have a show of hands on this question (pause). How many would use this computer if we buy it?" Then the chair announced the result. If a member had objected to this poll, the chair would have asked "All willing for this meeting to conduct this poll, please say 'yes'"(pause); "All opposed, please say 'no.'" The chair would then have conducted the poll or not as the meeting decided (**see page 17, under Motions and Decisions**).

Q28. *Can you give an example of how a higher law would modify a rule of order?*

A28. The rule on equal rights (**see page 13, Equal Rights**) gives each member one vote. However, in some jurisdictions, laws governing meetings of condominium owners give each member one vote for each condominium unit owned by that member. A member owning five units in the condominium complex has five votes. Similarly in a corporation's shareholders' meeting, votes are usually proportional to the number of voting shares owned.

Another example would be the rule on a tie vote (**see page 25, Tie Vote**). In some jurisdictions, for example in some condominium owners' bylaws, laws governing meetings give the chair of the meeting a tie-breaking vote in addition to the chair's original vote.

Q29. *Our board spent $7,000 on repairs to an elevator, claiming it was an emergency; but their spending limit was $2,000. Were they in order?*

A29. Yes. However, at the next regular or special meeting, the members must ratify this expenditure (**see page 29, Ratifying a Previous Decision**). Usually this motion is passed. If the motion to ratify the expenditure is not passed, then the members have lost confidence in that board, and an election must be called to have them replaced (see also on page 29).

Q30. *Will these rules work in conventions, conferences, and legislative assemblies?*

A30. Yes, they will work well in conjunction with the specific procedures and rules dealing with agendas, delegates, speaking orders and limits, voting methods, and the many details involved in the smooth operation of such events.

It is easy to modify these rules of order with a standing rule or bylaw to make them conform to special needs.

Q31. *Can a formal president present a motion to the meeting?*

A31. A chair can arrange for another member to present the motion if he or she is willing to stay uninvolved. Otherwise, the chair can ask the vice president, secretary, or another member to chair the meeting throughout this discussion and voting while she participates from the floor as a regular member (**see page 14, Formal Chair**).

Q32. *What can members do if they notice a bias in a chair or committee?*

A32. A member can raise a point of order and insist that the chair (or committee) allow fair discussion of both sides of an issue (**see page 23, Member's right to speak**). If there is formal chair, members must insist that the chair be impartial (**see page 14, Formal Chair**).

Sample Meeting

The following is an example of a meeting governed by the rules laid out in this book. This script of an imaginary meeting contains examples of how the rules work in awkward situations. Before reading it, we suggest you first read the *Rules* in Part 1 and the *Frequently Asked Questions* thoroughly to see that the rules are mostly common sense. Then this sample meeting will be more useful.

C = Chair	
M = Member	**Page references**

   C: Welcome! Let's open our meeting. Are there any changes to the agenda? M1? **p16**

M1: *I move that consideration of a fish pond be deleted from the agenda.*

M2: *I second the motion.*

C: It has been moved and seconded that consideration of a fish pond be deleted from the agenda.

> [Discussion]

C: Are you ready to vote now?   **p22**

> [Members call out "Let's vote now"]

C: Since we are ready to vote, will the secretary please read the motion.

> [Secretary reads the motion]   **p22**

C: All in favor of deleting the fish pond from the agenda, please raise a hand. ... All opposed, please raise a hand. ... Thank you. The vote is tied.   **p25**
   There are 40 affirmative votes and 40 negative votes, so the motion did not pass, and the agenda remains unchanged. The minutes of our last meeting have been circulated. Are there any changes or omissions? Yes, M3?

M3: *The meeting started at 7:30, not 8:00 p.m.*

C: Thank you M3. If there are no objections (pause), will the secretary please make that correction   **p17**

now. Are there further corrections? …
All in favor of adopting the minutes as
corrected, please raise a hand. … All
opposed, please raise a hand. … Thank
you. The minutes have been adopted as
corrected, and the secretary and I will
sign them now.   **p27**

C: The next item on the agenda is a report
from the executive board, to be read by
M4.

   [M4 reads the report]

M4: *I move that this report be adopted
   as read.*   **p28**

M5: *I second the motion.*

C: It has been moved and seconded that
the report be adopted as read. M6?

M6: *I don't think we should be bound by this
   report's recommendation that we change
   our management company.*
      *I suggest that M4 replace the word
   "adopted" with the word "received."*

C: M4, are you willing to make that
change?   **p20**

M4: *No. I do not wish to make that change.*

C: Yes, M6?

M6: *I move that we amend this motion by replacing the word "adopted" with the word "received."*   **p19**

M7: *I second the motion.*

C: It has been moved and seconded that we amend this motion by replacing the word "adopted" with the word "received" to prevent the members from being bound by the report's recommendations.

   [Discussion]

   [Members call out "Let's vote now"]

C: If there are no objections, we will vote now. All in favor of the amendment changing the word "adopted" to the word "received," please raise a hand. … All opposed, please raise a hand. … Thank you. The amendment did not pass, and now we must consider the original, unchanged, motion. Is there any further discussion? Since there is none, let's vote. All in favor of adopting the report as read, please raise a hand. … All opposed, please raise a hand. …

Thank you. The motion to adopt has been passed.

M8: *Ms. Chair. Point of order.* **p32**

C: Yes, M8?

M8: *That vote was so close. I request we vote again by ballot.*

C: I am satisfied the vote was correct. M8?

M8: *Well, I am not satisfied, and I move that we vote again by ballot!* **p24**

M9: *I second the motion.*

C: All in favor of voting again by ballot, please stand and remain standing until I say "thank you." Will the secretary please help me count? … Thank you. All opposed, please stand. Secretary, please help count again. … Thank you. The motion to vote again by ballot has been lost, 37 affirmative and 43 negative. So the original motion to adopt M4's report with its recommendations remains passed. The next item on the agenda is the fish pond. M10?

M10: *I move that we informally discuss the idea of a new fish pond for a few minutes now.* **p26**

M11: *I second the motion.*

C: All in favor of informally discussing the fish pond now please raise a hand. … All opposed please raise a hand.… Thank you. The motion has been passed, so we will now discuss this topic together informally.

   [Informal discussion]

M12: *Since we are not ready to make a motion on this topic yet, I move that we continue with the agenda now.*

M13: *I second the motion.*

C: All in favor of continuing with the agenda now, please raise a hand. … All opposed, please raise a hand. … Thank you. The motion has been passed. The next item arising from the minutes is the notice of motion made at our last meeting about painting our **p18** building. M14?

M14: *Because I believe this motion should have strong support from a large majority of members, it contains a special requirement. I move that we have all the exterior wood of our building*

*painted at a cost not to exceed $20,000
and that this motion require a 75 percent
affirmative vote to pass.*   **p25**

M15: *I second the motion.*

  C: Since members have been notified, this
motion complies with our bylaws and
is in order. Would the secretary please
read it.

    [Secretary reads the motion]

  C: M14, do you wish to speak to your
motion?

    [M14 speaks to the motion]

    [Discussion]

M14: *After hearing the discussion, I wish to
reword my motion to read: that we
have the exterior window frames of our
building painted at a cost not to exceed
$10,000, and that this motion require a
75% affirmative vote to pass.*

M16: *I second the motion.*

M17: *I object to this change in the motion.*

M18: *I also object to this change in the
motion.*   **p19**

C: Since there have been two objections, this motion cannot be changed with the mover's privilege, and the original motion is still the motion on the floor. M14?

M14: *I move that we amend the motion by replacing the words "all the wood on the exterior of our building" with "the exterior window frames" and the price of "$20,000" with "$10,000."*

M19: *I second the amendment.*   **p20**

C: The amendment is in order. Would the secretary please read the amendment to be sure we have it written correctly?

[Secretary reads the amendment]

C: The mover of the amendment may speak first.

[Discussion]

[Members call out "Let's vote now"]

C: Hearing no objection, let's vote now. Will the secretary please read the amendment?

[Secretary reads the amendment]

C: All in favor of the amendment, please raise a hand. ... All opposed, please raise a hand. ... Thank you. A majority are in favor, and the amendment has been passed. The newly amended motion is now the motion on the floor. Would the secretary please read this new motion?

[Secretary reads the motion]

[Discussion]

C: Is there any further discussion? Will the secretary please read the new motion again before we vote on it?

[Secretary reads the motion]

C: Does everyone understand what we are voting on? ... To make counting easy, we will have a standing vote. All in favor of the motion, please stand. ... All opposed, please stand. ...
Thank you.   **p24**
There were 48 affirmative votes and 32 negative votes, which means 60 percent are affirmative. The motion required 75% to pass. It has been lost. M20?

M20: *I move that we reconsider this motion.*   p27

M21: *I second the motion.*

  C: All in favor of reconsidering the motion, please raise a hand. … All opposed, please raise a hand. … A majority is in favor, and the motion to reconsider has been passed. M22?

M22: *With a slight modification, I think this idea might gain approval. I move that we have the exterior window frames and doors of the building painted at a cost not to exceed $15,000 and that this motion require a 75% affirmative vote to pass.*

M23: *I second the motion.*

  C: Would the secretary please read the motion.

     [Secretary reads the motion]

     [Discussion]

  C: M24?

M24: *Ms. Chair, I move we vote now.*

M25: *I second the motion.*

C: As soon as M26, who was waiting to speak, has had his turn, I will accept your motion.   **p23**

M26: *Thank you. [M26 speaks.]*

C: It has been moved and seconded that we vote now.

M28: *Ms. Chair, point of order. Several more of us would like to speak to this motion.*

C: Both sides of the question have been fairly presented during the past 20 minutes. Over 80 members are present. We will let the members decide.   **p26** All in favor of voting now, please raise a hand. ... All opposed, please raise a hand. ... Thank you. The motion is carried and we will vote now. Secretary, please read the motion once again.

   [Secretary reads the motion]

C: Thank you. We will have a standing vote. All in favor, please stand. ... Thank you. All opposed, please stand. ... Thank you. There were 60 affirmative votes and 20 negative votes. The number of affirmative votes was 75% of the total votes, so the motion has been passed. The executive board can now have this work done. Next on our agenda is new business. M29?

M29: *I move that we reconsider this last motion.*   **p27**

M30: *I second the motion.*

C: All in favor of reconsidering this last motion, please raise a hand. ... All opposed, please raise a hand. ... The motion to reconsider has been lost.

M30: *I move that we reconsider this last motion.*

M29: *I second the motion.*

C: This motion is out of order as we have already made a decision on it. M30?

M30: *Ms. Chair. It is not out of order, as our rules of order state on page 27 that "A motion can be reconsidered as often as the members are willing."*

C: The members have just decided that they are not willing to reconsider this motion, so we will now proceed with new business. M31?

M31: *My condominium is next to the games room, and players are frequently noisy. I move that this room be closed daily at 9:00 p.m.*

C: Is there a seconder for the motion? The motion fails for lack of a seconder. M32?   p17

M32: *I move that we post a sign in the games room asking players to be quiet after 9:00 p.m.*

M33: *I second the motion.*

C: It has been moved and seconded that we post a sign in the games room re-questing players to be quiet after 9:00 p.m. Is there any discussion?

M34: *The motion should put a limit on the cost of this sign.*

C: M32?

M32: *Good idea. I would like to change my motion to read that the maintenance committee be asked to spend up to $45 for a sign in the games room requesting players to be quiet after 9:00 p.m.*

M33: *I second the new motion.*

M35: *I object to this change in M32's original motion.*

C: Since there is only one objection, this change is acceptable. Will the secretary please read the new motion. **p19**

[Secretary reads the motion]

C: M36?

M36: *Because there are other factors to be considered, I move that we refer this motion to the executive board for their consideration and ask them to report back to us at our next meeting.* **p21**

M37: *I second the motion.*

[Discussion]

C: Anyone else? ... It has been moved and seconded that we refer this motion to the executive board and ask them to report back to us at our next meeting. All in favor, please raise a hand. ... All opposed, please raise a hand. ... The motion is carried. Is there any further new business? M38?

M38: *Three meetings ago we decided to carpet the foyer. Nothing has been done. I*

move that we rescind the motion to
carpet the foyer!   **p26**

M34: *I second the motion.*

M39: *Ms. Chair. Point of order.*

   C: Go ahead, M39.

M39: *The contract has been given to a firm.*
By our rules of order we cannot rescind
that motion.

   C: I believe you are right, M39. We cannot
rescind a motion if doing so would
create a breach of contract. M38?

M38: *The color is wrong! The price is too high!*
We are not breaking a contract! It hasn't
been signed yet! I insist that we—

M39: *I agree with—*

   C: Hold on a minute, M39! Please wait
until you have been acknowledged
before speaking.   **p15**

M38: *Ms. Chair. Point of order.*   **p32**

   C: Yes, M38.

M38: *I believe this motion is in order and*
request a vote on this point of order.

C: Thank you, M38. Please explain your reasoning. Then I will explain my reasoning, and then we will vote.

[M38 explains]

[C responds]

C: Now the members will decide. All who believe that this motion to rescind is out of order, please raise a hand. ... All opposed, please raise a hand. ... Thank you. The motion has been carried. The motion to rescind has been considered out of order, and we will now proceed to the next item of business.

[More business is discussed]

C: Our standing rules require us to adjourn by 10:00 p.m. We have only ten minutes left. M40?   **p29**

M40: *I move that we change that standing rule to read: "that we adjourn at 10:00 p.m. or at a later time if the members attending so wish."*

M41: *I second the motion.*

C: This motion, if passed, will not affect tonight's closing time as we are governed

by our existing standing rule. The
motion before us is that we
change our standing rule   **p10**
to read that "we adjourn at 10:00 p.m.
or at a later time if the members attending so wish."

[Short discussion]

[Members call out "Let's vote now"]

C: Secretary, please read the motion.

[Secretary reads the motion]

C: If there is no objection, we will vote
now. All in favor, please raise a hand.
… All opposed, please raise a hand. …
The motion has been carried and will
allow members to extend the time of
adjournment at future meetings. It is
now 10:00 p.m., and I declare this
meeting adjourned!

Flowchart

Using *Democratic Rules of Order*

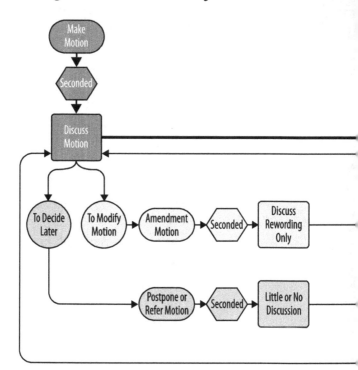

Good Order
- Stay on topic
- One speaker at a time, acknowledged by chair
- No interrupting

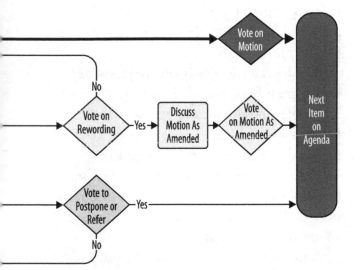

Point of Order
- Member explains how a law or good order
  is being breached
- Chair rules on point of order
- Vote if necessary

A printable color version of the Flowchart is available for
download here: democraticrules.com/pdf/flowchart.pdf

Summary of the Rules

A printable version of this Summary is available for download at democraticrules.com/pdf/summary.pdf

Fairness (equal rights of members) and good order are the underlying principles (**page 13**).

The **final authority is the majority of voting members,** provided a quorum is present, subject always to any applicable higher law (a law of the land, a constitution, a bylaw, or an existing standing rule) (**page 15**).

In **formal meetings**, the chair guides impartially without taking part in discussion. In **informal meetings**, the chair participates as an equal member (**page 14**).

A **motion** should be worded affirmatively and must not conflict with any higher law. Each motion requires a **seconder** (**page 17**).

The **mover's privilege** allows the mover to reword or withdraw the motion provided there is a seconder and not more than one member objects (**page 19**).

Amendments can delete, substitute, or add words to a motion on the floor but must not negate it or change its topic. An amendment cannot be amended (**page 20**).

Postpone, refer: A motion can be postponed to an indefinite or a specific future occasion or referred to a committee for further study (**page 21**).

Voting: Common voting methods include voting by ballot, standing, show of hands, show of voting cards, and voice. For a motion to pass, a quorum must be present, and more than half the votes cast must be affirmative (**pages 22 to 26**).

Informal discussion: A motion to informally discuss some topic, if passed, allows members to consider an idea without the formality of a motion (**page 26**).

Rescind, reconsider: A previous decision can be rescinded or reconsidered by the members at any appropriate time (**pages 26 and 27**).

Ratify a previous decision: A decision exceeding the authority of a member, committee or meeting can be ratified at a later meeting (**page 29**).

Good order: Members should discuss only one motion at a time. A member must not take more than a fair share of floor time nor interrupt another member except as allowed with a point of order (**page 32**).

Point of order: A member who believes that a law or the meeting's good order is being breached may rise immediately and say "point of order." The chair should allow the member to explain and, if necessary, should call for a vote for a decision (**page 32**).

Index

About the Authors

By 1994, when they wrote the first edition of *Democratic Rules of Order,* Fred and Peg Francis had had decades of experience with meetings in school, college, business, church, and community organizations as members and as officers. After attending university together, Peg taught elementary school. Fred taught mathematics in high schools and college. Together, they also designed several commercial products, including clean-burning wood stoves, rodent-proof composters, and children's building sets. For over 60 years, they lived in Victoria, Canada, where they raised four wonderful children and six equally wonderful grandchildren.

Since Fred's passing in 2003, Peg has continued their work in improving our democratic process. As the daughter of Fred and Peg Francis, Joyce McMenamon has been making her parents' book available through her Cool

Heads Publishing venture. Joyce is eager to share this valuable tool and to continue the work that Fred and Peg started.

This book was a very satisfying project for Fred and Peg, who saw the urgent need for more justice and stronger democracies in our world. For a democracy to work successfully, the populace itself must understand and want to obey the democratic principles. Citizens need practice in making the individual rights of each member and the rights of the majority work together. People using this book are learning and practicing these principles, and helping the world at the grassroots level.

May this book help you and your organization to have productive and distinctly democratic meetings!

—Fred and Peg Francis, Victoria, British Columbia, Canada

A Note about the Publisher

NEW SOCIETY PUBLISHERS is an activist, solutions-oriented publisher focused on publishing books for a world of change. Our books offer tips, tools, and insights from leading experts in sustainable building, homesteading, climate change, environment, conscientious commerce, renewable energy, and more — positive solutions for troubled times.

We're proud to hold to the highest environmental and social standards of any publisher in North America. This is why some of our books might cost a little more. We think it's worth it!

- We're carbon-neutral (since 2006)
- We're certified as a B Corporation (since 2016)
- Our corporate structure is an innovative employee shareholder agreement, so we're one-third employee-owned (since 2015)

At New Society Publishers, we care deeply about *what* we publish —but also about *how* we do business.

Download our catalogue at https://newsociety.com/Our-Catalog or for a printed copy please email info@newsocietypub.com.

www.newsociety.com

9 780865 719064